The Sayings of Jonathan Swift

The Sayings of

JONATHAN
SWIFT

edited by
JOSEPH SPENCE

DUCKWORTH

First published in 1994 by
Gerald Duckworth & Co. Ltd.
The Old Piano Factory
48 Hoxton Square, London N1 6PB
Tel: 071 729 5986
Fax: 071 729 0015

Introduction and editorial arrangement
© 1994 by Joseph Spence

A catalogue record for this book is available
from the British Library

ISBN 0 7156 2633 7

Typeset by Ray Davies
Printed in Great Britain by
Redwood Books Ltd., Trowbridge

Contents

For Kitty, William and James.

Introduction

Jonathan Swift lies buried in a tomb in St Patrick's Cathedral in Dublin, under what Yeats called 'the greatest epitaph in history'. About that we can be certain, but there are mysteries, doubts, conundrums and paradoxes surrounding almost every other stage and facet of Swift's life. He set a number of false scents himself. Contemporaries and later critics, benign and malign, have ensured that there are tortuous trails for his biographers to follow.

It is believed that Jonathan Swift was born in Dublin on 30 November 1667. He was probably the posthumous son of a young man of Yorkshire descent, whose minor gentry family had recently settled in Ireland. There was some talk, in his lifetime, that Swift may have been the illegitimate child of his first patron, Sir William Temple. But more sensational than this gossip was a story of infant abduction which Swift related in a fragment of autobiography, written towards the end of his life. This episode reads like a scene from Laurence Sterne's picaresque classic, *Tristram Shandy*, with resonances of *The Importance of Being Earnest*. It is, therefore, a wonderfully apposite first adventure to find in the life story of an author often portrayed as the father of Anglo-Irish literature.

Swift recorded that when he was about twelve months old he was stolen by his nurse, who was besotted with him, and taken from Dublin to the north of England. Here he was to remain for nearly three years, because his mother, Abigail (of whom he professed to be fonder than of any other of his kin), considered a return voyage too hazardous for the child. Thus the infant Jonathan laid himself open to Lady

Bracknell's famous charge: 'To lose one parent may be regarded as a misfortune; to lose both looks like carelessness.' However, Swift recorded that by the time he was returned to his mother he could read any chapter of the Bible, so all may have been for the best.

There is also uncertainty, if not deliberate carelessness, in Swift's accounts of his position in the household of Sir William Temple at Moor Park in the 1690s. He always described himself as Temple's personal secretary, but whether he was hired help, brilliant protégé or surrogate son remains unclear. Swift's sensitive spirit certainly led him to feel that he was frequently slighted and undervalued, but from the time of the death of his patron, in 1699, he was more often to boast of having enjoyed a real intimacy with Sir William.

It is no easier to gauge the precise relationship between Swift and the great Tory statesmen with whom he was conversant, socially and politically, in his London years (1710-13). He will always be celebrated by men of letters for having wielded the pen which broke the sword of the Duke of Marlborough in 1710, for few pamphleteers have had so direct an effect on public affairs as Swift had with *The Conduct of the Allies* and his articles for *The Examiner*. However, doubts remain as to whether he was ever fully in the confidence of St John and Harley, and allowed to share the deeper secrets of state, or whether he was simply a good hack, taken up for a season, out of necessity, and then rewarded with a position in his native Dublin, where he was to spend the rest of his life.

Again Swift felt slighted, but while he portrayed his appointment as Dean of St Patrick's in 1713 as a form of banishment, his patrons saw it as precisely the sort of placing his short service work for the Tory cause deserved. Swift continued to make much of his close propinquity to power in the last years of Queen Anne's reign, but he was probably as guilty of mild delusions of grandeur, and of the sin of pride, as any of the contemporaries he mocked for those vices. Indeed, his poetic reflections on his public role in 'The Author Upon Himself ' (1714) are embarrassingly, but unconsciously, honest in revealing him as a sort of higher servant, pathetically proud of lesser servants' shows of deference towards him.

In Swift's private life there are even greater mysteries. The most widely debated of these is that surrounding his relationship with 'Stella' (Esther Johnson), Sir William Temple's beautiful and intelligent ward, with whom he had established a friendship when she was a young girl at Moor Park. Swift wrote some of his best poems on the occasions of her birthday and the *Journal to Stella* (1710-13) remains one of the most intriguing records of the social aspect of high-political life. He also wrote most movingly of her in a testament composed at the time of her death. However, these sources do not reveal the secret of their personal relationship. That 'Stella' followed him to Dublin in 1701 is known, but whether they were ever married or whether they consummated their long 'affair' are subjects still open to conjecture. Indeed, all of Swift's affairs of the heart, and especially his relationships with 'Vanessa' (Esther Vanhomrigh) and 'Varina' (Jane Waring), have raised questions. What his re-christening of his favourite women betrays, however, is that Swift was happier dealing with them at a distance and in idealised form, under classical nomenclature, rather than as flesh and blood creatures, likely to refuse his demands or make demands of their own. As one critic has recently put it, Swift was always caught between idealising women as 'angels in petticoats' and feeling repelled by them as 'beasts in skirts'.

On the subject of Ireland, Swift declared his views more plainly, but there is continuing debate as to whether one can take his professed loathing of the country and its people at face value. Acknowledgment of the ambivalence or 'double vision' of the Anglo-Irish in their attitude towards Ireland is now commonplace. Swift's particular 'double vision' took the form of seeing most things from the point of view of the Englishman, while playing at being an Irishman when exposing English perfidy in Ireland, most famously when he adopted the persona of the Drapier, in his assault on Wood's halfpence in 1724. However, whatever the psychological motivation for his disguise, Swift committed himself to particular Irish causes with a martyr-like zeal, which made him the toast of the Dublin poor. He may have argued that he championed human liberty rather than Irish nationality, but in *A Modest Proposal* and the *Drapier's Letters*, at least, Ireland found one of her most able and ardent defenders.

The ambivalence of Swift's attitude to Ireland is most clearly seen in his view of the native Irish Catholics. He often condemned them for a multiplicity of vices, but he also admitted that they had a certain vitality of which he – the repressed Protestant searcher after Reason – was deeply envious. Thus, when in *Gulliver's Travels* the eponymous hero is bewailing the unteachability of the Yahoo (Man), he observes, with a reference which can only be to the native Irish, that 'the red-haired of both sexes are more libidinous and mischievous than the rest, whom they yet much exceed in strength and activity'. Of course, there is a larger point at issue here than Swift's view of the Irish. *Gulliver's Travels* has passed down to us as a children's classic, but it is one of the great source books for Swift's philosophy of man, being the work in which he sought to vex, and mend, the world, with the revelation that man is not so much a rational being as an animal capable of reasoning.

Whether Swift was capable of reasoning in his later years or whether he was certifiably mad is the last of the long line of queries one has to tackle in trying to make sense of his life and character. It is a nice touch that it was Oscar Wilde's father, Sir William Wilde, the eminent Dublin surgeon, who in 1849 launched an early defence of Swift against the charge of lunacy. However, Wilde's conjectures were pretty wide of the mark and his sources largely literary. His book represented a defence of Irish nationality against English and Scottish asperity rather than a defence of Swift based on sustained medical research. It was left to modern experts to bury the myth of 'the Mad Dean', which had been popularised by Dr Johnson and Sir Walter Scott, and to promote the idea that Swift was not insane but simply continuing to suffer, and now more aggravatedly, from the Meniere's disease he had developed in young manhood.

When one turns from looking at Swift the man to examining his works, one is on surer ground, although the opinions and beliefs of the natural ironist are never easy to decipher. What is indisputable is the extent of Swift's literary achievement. Even among the great literary figures of the first half of the eighteenth century – Pope, Congreve and Gay in poetry and drama; Addison and Steele in prose – Swift stood like a colossus. He has always been a controversial subject, and major critics of every age have found some of his meat rather too strong for them, but few have failed to admire the clarity and directness of his prose and the sharpness of his wit. He also managed to be a more important public man than any of his literary peers, for one does sense that, if he was never quite as close to the hub of power as he would have liked his readers to believe, he was, nevertheless, close enough to be able to offer some wise reflections on the world of high politics.

More than any other writer in the English language, Swift made irony and satire respectable – and formidable. He was the greatest enemy of cant and hypocrisy in his age and a coruscating critic of flaccid liberal thinking, weak-mindedness and fudge. He was a stern and effective moralist, but also a kindlier and more humorous observer of the human condition than has sometimes been thought. He was not a bitter misanthrope, disappointed in public and private life, but someone who was loyal to those he loved and who forgave as many foibles as he damned. It is true that he saw life as a constant battle between Reason and Nature, but he seldom failed to acknowledge that battle had its comic as well as its tragic aspect. This becomes evident in such works as his *Advice to Servants* and his *Polite Conversation*. These gentler productions of the 1730s reveal that his ear for the absurdities and crass social niceties of Augustan London was as keen as that of the great observers of succeeding generations, Oliver Goldsmith and Richard Brinsley Sheridan. Thus Jonathan Swift takes his place at the head of the apostolic succession of Anglo-Irish critics of English life, which leads beyond Goldsmith and Sheridan to Bernard Shaw and, of course, Oscar Wilde.

Note on sources

The quotations which follow are given in chronological order, with the exception of the many which derive from Swift's *Thoughts on Various Subjects*. These aphorisms, collected over the course of his life (and published in 1711, 1727 and posthumously in 1745), are offered here at the beginning of each section.

Swift on Swift

I drink little, miss my glass often, put water in my wine, and go away before the rest, which I take to be a good receipt for sobriety. Let us put it into rhyme, and so make a proverb:

> Drink little at a time:
> Put water with your wine;
> Miss your glass when you can;
> And go off the first man.

Journal to Stella, 21 April 1711

I love good creditable acquaintance; I love to be the worst of the company: I am not of those that say, for want of company, welcome trumpery.

ibid., 17 May 1711

The public is a very civil person, and I am its humble servant, but I shall be glad to shake hands with it as soon as I can. Letter to Charles Ford, 8 September 1711

Swift had the sin of wit, no venial crime ...

And now, the public interest to support,
By Harley Swift invited comes to court.
In favour grows with ministers of state;
Admitted private, when superiors wait:
And, Harley, not ashamed his choice to own,
Takes him to Windsor in his coach, alone.
At Windsor Swift no sooner can appear,
But, St.John comes and whispers in his ear;
The waiters stand in ranks; the yeomen cry,
'Make room', as if a duke were passing by.

By faction tired, with grief he waits a while,
His great contending friends to reconcile.
Performs what friendship, justice, truth require:
What could he more, but decently retire?

'The Author Upon Himself', 1714

I have ever hated all nations, professions and communities, and all my love is towards individuals ... I hate and detest that animal called man; although I heartily love John, Peter, Thomas and so forth. This is the system upon which I have governed myself many years.

Letter to Alexander Pope, 29 September 1725

[M]y greatest misery is recollecting the scene of twenty years past, and then all of a sudden dropping into the present. I remember when I was a little boy, I felt a great fish at the end of my line which I drew up almost on the ground, but it dropped in, and the disappointment vexeth me to this very day, and I believe was the type of all my future disappointments.

Letter to Viscount Bolingbroke, 5 April 1729

Fair LIBERTY was all his cry ...

Had he but spared his tongue and pen,
He might have rose like other men:
But, power was never in his thought;
And, wealth he valued not a groat ...

Perhaps I may allow the Dean
Had too much satire in his vein;
And seemed determined not to starve it,
Because no age could more deserve it.
Yet, malice never was his aim;
He lashed the vice, but spared the name;
No individual could resent,
Where thousands equally were meant.
His satire points at no defect,
But what all mortals may correct.

He gave the little wealth he had,
To build a house for fools and mad;
And showed by one satiric touch,
No nation wanted it so much:
That kingdom he hath left his debtor,
I wish it soon may have a better.

'Verses on the Death of Doctor Swift', 1731

I do not think life is of much value, but health is worth
everything ... For my own part I labour for daily health
as often and almost as many hours as a workman does
for daily bread, and like a common labourer can but just
earn enough to keep life and soul together. I had almost
as lieve plough as ride, and thresh as walk, if by any
expense within my power I could contrive, that laziness
would do me no hurt. You see I have the common folly
of quoting myself. But I think it almost the only thing I
am right in; and God knows, it is with great force that I
reason myself into the practice.

Letter to Charles Ford, 9 December 1732

Deaf, giddy, odious to my friends,
Now all my consolation ends;
No more I hear my church's bell
Than if it rang out for my knell.

'On his Own Deafness', 1734

'I'll send you my bill of fare,' said Lord Bolingbroke,
when trying to persuade Dr Swift to dine with him.
– 'Send me your bill of company,' was Swift's answer to
him.

Quoted in Joseph Spence's *Anecdotes*

The Nature of Man

Ambition often puts men upon doing the meanest offices; so climbing is performed in the same posture with creeping.

Thoughts on Various Subjects

Some people take more care to hide their wisdom than their folly.

ibid.

I never wonder to see men wicked, but I often wonder to see them unashamed.

ibid.

Most sorts of diversion in men, children, and other animals, are an imitation of fighting.

ibid.

Very few men, properly speaking, live at present, but are providing to live another time.

ibid.

How inconsistent is man with himself!

ibid.

I never yet knew a wag ... who was not a dunce.

ibid.

A man should never be ashamed to own he has been in the wrong, which is but saying, in other words, that he is wiser today than he was yesterday.

ibid.

Men are contented to be laughed at for their wit, but not for their folly.

ibid.

A nice man is a man of nasty ideas.

ibid.

I must complain the cards are ill shuffled, till I have a good hand.

ibid.

How is it possible to expect mankind will take advice, when they will not so much as take warning?

ibid.

No man will take counsel, but every man will take money: therefore money is better than counsel.

ibid.

Lions, bears, elephants, and some other animals, are strong or valiant, and their species never degenerate in their native soil, except they happen to be enslaved or destroyed by human fraud. But men degenerate every day, merely by the folly, the perverseness, the avarice, the tyranny, the pride, the treachery, or inhumanity of their own kind.

Thoughts on Religion, undated

And pray, what is man, but a topsyturvy creature, his animal faculties perpetually mounted on his rational, his head where his heels should be, grovelling on the earth! And yet with all his faults, he sets up to be an universal reformer and corrector of abuses, a remover of grievances, rakes into every slut's corner of Nature, bringing hidden corruptions to the light, and raises a mighty dust where there was none before; sharing deeply all the while in the very same pollutions he pretends to sweep away.

A Meditation Upon a Broomstick, 1701

As wit is the noblest and most useful gift of human nature, so humour is the most agreeable.

'An Apology', *A Tale of a Tub,* 1709

Human nature seems to be under this disadvantage, that
the example alone of a vicious Prince will in time
corrupt an age; but the example of a good one will not
be sufficient to reform it without further endeavours.

A Project for the Advancement of Religion, 1709

I never expect sincerity from any man; and am no more
angry at the breach of it, than at the colour of his hair.

Letter to Charles Ford, 8 September 1711

When you are melancholy, read diverting or amusing
books; it is my receipt, and seldom fails. Health, good
humour, and fortune, are all that is valuable in this life,
and the last contributes to the two former.

Letter to Esther Vanhomrigh, 7 August 1722

Expect no more from man than such an animal is
capable of, and you will everyday find my description of
Yahoos more resembling. You should think and deal
with every man as a villain, without calling him so, or
flying from him, or valuing him less. This is an old true
lesson.

Letter to Thomas Sheridan, 11 September 1725

I have got materials towards a treatise proving the
falsity of that definition *animal rationale*; and to show it
should be only *rationis capax*. Upon this great foundation
of misanthropy ... the whole building of my [Gulliver's]
Travels is erected.

Letter to Alexander Pope, 29 September 1725

Men are never so serious, thoughtful, and intent, as
when they are at stool.

Gulliver's Travels III, 1726

I never wake without finding life a more insignificant
thing than it was the day before.

Letter to Viscount Bolingbroke, 5 April 1729

All human race would fain be wits,
And millions miss for one that hits.

'On Poetry: A Rhapsody', 1733

A mingled mass of good and bad;
The best and worst that may be had.

ibid.

But Man we find the only creature,
Who, led by Folly, fights with Nature.

ibid.

The Way of the World

Life is not a farce, it is a ridiculous tragedy, which is the worst kind of composition.

Thoughts on Various Subjects

There are but three ways for a man to revenge himself of a censorious world. To despise it; to return the like; or to endeavour to live so as to avoid it. The first of these is usually pretended; the last is almost impossible; the universal practice is for the second.

ibid.

It is pleasant to observe how free the present age is in laying taxes on the next. *Future ages shall talk of this. This shall be famous to all posterity.* Whereas, their time and thoughts will be taken up about present things, as ours are now.

ibid.

When a true genius appears in the world, you may know him by this sign, that the dunces are all in confederacy against him.

ibid.

When the world has once begun to use us ill, it afterwards continues the same treatment with less scruple or ceremony, as men do a whore.

ibid.

Life is a tragedy wherein we sit as spectators for a while and then act our part in it.

ibid.

The latter part of a wise man's life is taken up in curing the follies, prejudices, and false opinions he had contracted in the former.

ibid.

The power of fortune is confessed only by the miserable; for the happy impute all their success to prudence or merit.

ibid.

As universal a practice as lying is, and as easy a one as it seems, I do not remember to have heard three good lies in all my conversation, even from those who were most celebrated in that faculty.

ibid.

Although reason were intended by Providence to govern our passions, yet it seems that, in two points of the greatest moment to the being and continuance of the world, God hath intended our passions to prevail over our reason. The first is, the propagation of our species, since no wise man ever married from the dictates of reason. The other is, the love of life, which, from the dictates of reason, every man would despise, and wish it at an end, or that it never had a beginning.

Thoughts on Religion, undated

There is nothing in this world constant, but inconstancy.

A Tritical Essay upon the Faculties of the Mind, 1709

The Scripture tells us, that 'oppression makes a wise man mad'. Therefore, consequently speaking, the reason why some men are not mad is because they are not wise. However, it were to be wished that oppression would in time teach a little wisdom to fools.

Proposal for the Universal Use of Irish Manufacture, 1720

[On lawyers:] I said there was a society of men among us, bred up from their youth in the art of proving by words multiplied for the purpose, that white is black, and black is white, according as they are paid. To this society all the rest of the people are slaves ... Here my master, interposing, said it was a pity, that creatures endowed with such prodigious abilities of mind ... were not rather encouraged to be instructors of others in wisdom and knowledge. In answer to which, I assured his Honour, that in all points out of their own trade they were usually the most ignorant and stupid generation among us, the most despicable in common conversation, avowed enemies to all knowledge and learning, and equally disposed to pervert the general reason of mankind in every other subject of discourse, as in that of their own profession.

Gulliver's Travels IV, 1726

Manners & Conversation

Good manners is the art of making those people easy with whom we converse.

Treatise on Good Manners and Good Breeding, undated

As the best law is founded upon reason, so are the best manners.

ibid.

Pride, ill-nature, and want of sense, are the three great sources of ill-manners.

ibid.

I defy any one to assign an incident wherein reason will not direct us what we are to say or to do in company, if we are not misled by pride or ill-nature.

ibid.

Good sense is the principal foundation of good manners.

ibid.

There is a pedantry in manners, as in all arts and sciences; and sometimes in trades. Pedantry is properly the overrating any kind of knowledge we pretend to.

ibid.

Nothing is so great an instance of ill-manners as flattery. If you flatter all the company, you please none; if you flatter only one or two, you affront the rest.

Hints on Good Manners, undated

Good conversation is not to be expected in much company, because few listen, and there is continual interruption. But good or ill manners are discovered let the company be ever so large.

ibid.

Flattery is the worst, and falsest way of shewing our esteem.

ibid.

Courts are the worst of all schools to teach good manners.

ibid.

Good manners chiefly consist in action, not in words. Modesty and humility the chief ingredients.

ibid.

Argument ... is the worst sort of conversation; as it is generally in books the worst sort of reading.

ibid.

Perpetual aiming at wit, a very bad part of conversation. It is done to support a character. It generally fails. It is a sort of insult on the company, and a constraint upon the speaker.

ibid.

For a man to talk in his own trade, or business, or faculty, is a great breach of good manners. Divines, physicians, lawyers, soldiers, particularly poets, are frequently guilty of this weakness.

ibid.

Pedantry is the too frequent or unseasonable obtruding of our own knowledge in common discourse, and placing a too great value upon it.

Towards an Essay on Conversation, 1710

The worst conversation I ever remember to have heard in my life, was that of Wills' coffee house, where the wits (as they were called) used formerly to assemble; that is to say, five or six men who had writ plays, or at least prologues, or had a share in a miscellany, came thither, and entertained one another with their trifling composures, in so important an air, as if they had been the noblest efforts of human nature, or that the fate of kingdoms depended on them.

ibid.

Raillery is the finest part of conversation; but, as it is our usual custom to counterfeit and adulterate whatever is dear to us, so we have done with this, and turned it all into what is generally called repartee, or being smart.

ibid.

Nothing hath spoiled men more for conversation, than the character of being wits, to support which, they never fail of encouraging a number of followers and admirers, who list themselves in their service, wherein they find their accounts on both sides, by pleasing their mutual vanity.

ibid.

The flowers of wit, fancy, wisdom, humour, and politeness, scattered in this volume, amount to one thousand, seventy and four. Allowing then to every gentleman and lady thirty visiting families ... there will want but a little of an hundred polite questions, answers, replies, rejoinders, repartees, and remarks, to be daily delivered fresh, in every company, for twelve solar months ... I am altogether for exalting this science to its utmost perfection.

A Complete Collection of Genteel and Ingenious Conversation
According to the Most Polite Mode and Method Now Used at
Court, and in the Best Companies of England
(henceforth *Polite Conversation*), 1737-8

A footman may swear; but he cannot swear like a lord. He can swear as often: but can he swear with equal delicacy, propriety, and judgment? No, certainly, unless he be a lad of superior parts, of good memory, a diligent observer; one who hath a skilful ear, some knowledge in music, and an exact taste, which hardly falls to the share of one in a thousand among that fraternity, in as high favour as they now stand with their ladies ... [T]he waiting-woman ... if she hath been bred to read romances, may have some small subaltern, or second-hand politeness; and if she constantly attends the tea, and be a good listener, may, in some years, make a tolerable figure, which will serve, perhaps, to draw in the young chaplain or the old steward. But, alas! after all, how can she acquire those hundreds of graces and motions, and airs, the whole military management of the fan, the contortions of every muscular motion in the face, the risings and fallings, the quickness and slackness of the voice, with the several tones and cadences; the proper junctures of smiling and frowning, how often and how loud to laugh, when to gibe and when to flout, with all the other branches of doctrine and discipline above recited? *ibid.*

Lady Smart: Ladies and gentlemen, will you eat any oysters before dinner?

Colonel: With all my heart. [Takes an oyster.] He was a bold man, that first ate an oyster.

Lady S: They say, oysters are a cruel meat, because we eat them alive. Then they are an uncharitable meat, for we leave nothing to the poor; and they are an ungodly meat, because we never say grace to them.

Neverout: Faith, that's as well said, as if I had said it myself.

Lady S: Well, we are well set, if we be as well served. Come, Colonel, handle your arms; shall I help you to some beef?

Col.: If your ladyship pleases; and, pray, don't cut like a mother-in-law, but send me a large slice; for I love a good foundation. *ibid.*, Dialogue II

Women, Love & Marriage

When a man pretends love, but courts for money, he is like a juggler, who conjures away your shilling, and conveys something very indecent under the hat.

Thoughts on Various Subjects

What they do in heaven we are ignorant of; what they do *not* we are told expressly, that they neither marry, nor are given in marriage.

ibid.

The reason why so few marriages are happy is because young ladies spend their time in making nets, not in making cages.

ibid.

A very little wit is valued in a woman, as we are pleased with a few words spoken plain by a parrot.

ibid.

I have known men of valour, cowards to their wives.

ibid.

Matrimony hath many children; repentance, discord, poverty, jealousy, sickness, spleen, loathing, &c.

ibid.

Venus, a beautiful good-natur'd lady, was the Goddess of Love; Juno, a terrible shrew, the Goddess of Marriage; and they were always mortal enemies.

ibid.

Now hardly here and there an hackney-coach
Appearing, show'd the ruddy morn' approach.
Now Betty from her master's bed had flown,
And softly stole to discompose her own.

'A Description of the Morning', April 1709

The other day we had a long discourse with [Lady Orkney] about love; and she told us a saying ... which I thought excellent, that in men, desire begets love, and in women that love begets desire.

Journal to Stella, 30 October 1712

Love, why do we one passion call?
When 'tis a compound of them all;
Where hot and cold, where sharp and sweet,
In all their equipages meet;
Where pleasures mixed with pains appear,
Sorrow with joy, and hope with fear.

'Cadenus and Vanessa', *c.* 1712

Love with white lead cements its wings,
White lead was sent us to repair
Two brightest, brittlest, earthly things,
A lady's face, and china-ware.

'The Progress of Beauty', 1719

It is usual in young wives before they have been many weeks married, to assume a bold, forward look and manner of talking; as if they intended to signify in all companies, that they were no longer girls, and consequently that their whole demeanour, before they got a husband, was all but a countenance and constraint upon their nature.

A Letter to a Young Lady, on her Marriage, 1723

I advise that your company at home should consist of men, rather than women. To say the truth, I never yet knew a tolerable woman to be fond of her own sex [and] a knot of ladies, got together by themselves, is a very school of impertinence and detraction.

ibid.

There is never wanting in this town, a tribe of bold, swaggering, rattling ladies, whose talents pass among coxcombs for wit and humour ... I would recommend you to the acquaintance of a common prostitute, rather than to that of such termagants as these.

ibid.

The caprices of womankind are not limited by any
climate or nation.

Gulliver's Travels IV, 1726

Nor do they trust their tongue alone,
But speak a language of their own;
Can read a nod, a shrug, a look,
Far better than a printed book;
Convey a libel in a frown,
And wink a reputation down.

'The Journal of a Modern Lady', 1729

Poor ladies! though their business be to play,
'Tis hard they must be busy night and day:
Why should they want the privilege of men,
And take some small diversions now and then?
Had women been the makers of our laws;
(And why they were not I can see no cause;)
The men should slave at cards from morn to night;
And female pleasures be to read and write.

'The Hardship Put Upon Ladies', 1733

Bachelor's fare: bread and cheese and kisses.

Polite Conversation, Dialogue I, 1738

Under an oak in stormy weather,
I joined this rogue and whore together;
And none but he who rules the thunder
Can put this rogue and whore asunder.

Attrib.: a 'certificate' Swift wrote for an itinerant couple
he met and married upon the road to Lichfield

Servants

Never submit to stir a finger in any business, but that for which you were particularly hired. For example, if the groom be drunk or absent, and the butler be ordered to shut the stable door, the answer is ready, 'An please your honour, I don't understand horses.'

Directions to Servants, 1745

Write your own name and your sweetheart's, with the smoke of the candle, on the roof of the kitchen or the servants' hall, to show your learning.

ibid.

If you are a young, sightly fellow, whenever you whisper your mistress at the table, run your nose full in her cheek, or if your breath be good, breathe full in her face; this I know to have had very good consequences in some families.

ibid.

Never come till you have been called three or four times; for none but dogs will come at the first whistle; and when the master calls 'Who's there?', no servant is bound to come; for Who's there is nobody's name.

ibid.

Although you are allowed knives for the servants' hall at meals, yet you ought to spare them, and make use only of your master's.

ibid.

If it be possible, never tell a lie to your master or lady, unless you have some hopes that they cannot find it out in less than half an hour.

ibid.

Whoever comes to visit your master or lady when they are abroad, never burthen your memory with the person's name, for indeed you have too many other things to remember. Besides, it is a porter's business, and your master's fault that he doth not keep one; and who can remember names? and you will certainly mistake them, and you can neither write nor read.

ibid.

When a servant is turned off, all his faults must be told, although most of them were never known by his master or lady; and all mischiefs done by others, charge to him. And when they ask any of you why you never acquainted them before, the answer is, 'Sir, (or Madam) really I was afraid it would make you angry; and besides, perhaps you might think it was malice in me.'

ibid.

Where there are little masters and misses in a house, they are usually great impediments to the diversions of the servants; the only remedy is to bribe them with goody goodies, that they may not tell tales to papa and mamma.

If you be sent with ready money to buy anything at a shop, and happen at that time to be out of pocket (which is very usual), sink the money and take up the goods on your master's account. This is for the honour of your master and yourself; for he becomes a man of credit at your recommendation.

ibid.

If your master or lady happen once in their lives to accuse you wrongfully, you are a happy servant; for you have nothing more to do, than for every fault you commit while you are in their service, to put them in mind of that false accusation, and protest yourself equally innocent in the present case.

ibid.

When you invite the neighbouring servants to junket
with you at home in an evening, teach them a peculiar
way of tapping or scraping at the kitchen-window,
which you may hear, but not your master or lady, whom
you must take care not to disturb or frighten at such
unseasonable hours.   *ibid.*

Lay all faults on a lap dog, a favourite cat, a monkey, a
parrot, a child, or on a servant who was last turned off;
by this rule you will excuse yourself, do no hurt to any
body else, and save your master or lady from the trouble
and vexation of chiding.   *ibid.*

[To the Nurse:] If you happen let the child fall, and lame
it, be sure never confess it; if it dies, all is safe.

ibid.

[To the Footman:] In order to learn the secrets of other
families, tell them those of your master's; thus you will
grow a favourite both at home and abroad, and be
regarded as a person of importance.

ibid.

Learn all the new-fashion words, and oaths, and songs,
and scraps of plays, that your memory can hold. Thus
you will become the delight of nine ladies in ten, and the
envy of ninety-nine beaux in a hundred.

ibid.

When you are sent on a message, deliver it in your own
words, although it be to a duke or duchess, and not in
the words of your master or lady; for how can they
understand what belongs to a message as well as you,
who have been bred to the employment? But never
deliver the answer until it is called for, and then adorn it
with your own style.   *ibid.*

When you carry a dish of meat, dip your fingers in the
sauce, or lick it with your tongue, to try whether it be
good, and fit for your master's table.

ibid.

While grace is saying after meat, do you and your brethren take the chairs from behind the company, so that when they go to sit again, they may fall backwards, which will make them all merry; but be you so discreet as to hold your laughter till you get to the kitchen, and then divert your fellow-servants.

ibid.

The last advice I give you, relates to your behaviour when you are going to be hanged; which ... may very probably be your lot, and is owing to one of these three qualities; either a love of good fellowship, a generosity of mind, or too much vivacity of spirits. Your good behaviour on this article will concern your whole community ... Get a speech to be written by the best author of Newgate, some of your kind wenches will supply you with a Holland shirt, and white cap, crowned with a crimson or black ribbon: take leave cheerfully of all your friends in Newgate; mount the cart with courage; fall on your knees; lift up your eyes: hold a book in your hands, although you cannot read a word; deny the fact at the gallows; kiss and forgive the hangman, and so farewell: you shall be buried in pomp at the charge of the fraternity: the surgeons shall not touch a limb of you; and your fame shall continue until a successor of equal renown succeeds in your place.

ibid.

Whereas the bearer served me the space of one year, during which time he was an idler and a drunkard; I then discharged him as such; but how far his having been five years at sea may have mended his manners, I leave to the penetration of those who may hereafter chuse to employ him.

Certificate to a discarded servant, January 1739

Religion

We have just enough religion to make us hate, but not enough to make us love one another.

Thoughts on Various Subjects

Religion seems to have grown an infant with age, and requires miracles to nurse it, as it had in its infancy.

ibid.

Some men under the notion of weeding out prejudice, eradicate virtue, honesty, and religion.

ibid.

Complaint is the largest tribute Heaven receives, and the sincerest part of our devotion. *ibid.*

When men grow virtuous in their old age, they only make a sacrifice to God of the devil's leavings.

ibid.

The motives of the best actions will not bear too strict an enquiry. It is allowed, that the cause of most actions, good or bad, may be resolved into the love of ourselves; but the self-love of some men, inclines them to please others; and the self-love of others is wholly employed in pleasing themselves. This makes the great distinction between virtue and vice. Religion is the best motive of all actions, yet religion is allowed to be the highest instance of self-love. *ibid.*

Query, Whether churches are not dormitories of the living as well as of the dead? *ibid.*

Laws penned with the utmost care and exactness, and in the vulgar language, are often perverted to wrong meanings; then why should we wonder that the Bible is so? *ibid.*

Since the unity of divinity and humanity is the great article of our religion, it is odd to see some clergymen in their writings of divinity, wholly devoid of humanity.

ibid.

The preaching of divines helps to preserve well-inclined men in the course of virtue, but seldom or never reclaims the vicious.

ibid.

To say a man is bound to believe, is neither truth nor sense.

Thoughts on Religion, undated

You may force men, by interest or punishment, to say or swear they believe, and act as if they believed. You can go no further.

ibid.

Every man, as a member of the commonwealth, ought to be content with the possession of his own opinion in private, without perplexing his neighbour or disturbing the public.

ibid.

I look upon myself, in the capacity of a clergyman, to be one appointed by Providence for defending a post assigned to me, and for gaining over as many enemies as I can. Although I think my cause is just, yet one great motive is my submitting to the pleasure of providence, and to the laws of my country.

ibid.

Violent zeal for truth hath an hundred to one odds to be either petulancy, ambition, or pride.

ibid.

The Christian religion, in the most early times, was proposed to the Jews and heathens without the article of Christ's divinity; which, I remember, Erasmus accounts for, by its being too strong a meat for babes. Perhaps, if it were now softened by the Chinese missionaries, the conversion of those infidels would be less difficult ... But, in a country already Christian, to bring so fundamental a point of faith into debate, can have no consequences that are not pernicious to morals and public peace.

ibid.

God's mercy is over all His works, but divines of all
sorts lessen that mercy too much.   *ibid.*

I am not answerable to God for the doubts that arise in
my own breast, since they are the consequence of that
reason that He hath planted in me; if I take care to
conceal those doubts from others, if I use my best
endeavours to subdue them, and if they have no
influence on the conduct of my life.

ibid.

I believe that thousands of men would be orthodox
enough in certain points, if divines had not been too
curious, or too narrow, in reducing orthodoxy within the
compass of subtleties, niceties, and distinctions, with
little warrant from Scripture and less from reason or
good policy.   *ibid.*

Miserable mortals! Can we contribute to the honour and
glory of God? I wish that expression were struck out of
our Prayer-books.

ibid.

I never saw, heard, nor read, that the clergy were
beloved in any nation where Christianity was the
religion of the country. Nothing can render them
popular, but some degree of persecution.

ibid.

The last fanatics of note were those which started up in
Germany a little after the reformation of Luther,
springing as mushrooms do at the end of a harvest ...
[Their] visions and revelations always terminated in
leading about half a dozen sisters apiece, and making
that practice a fundamental part of their system. For
human life is a continual navigation, and if we expect
our vessels to pass safely through the waves and
tempests of this fluctuating world, it is necessary to
make a good provision of the flesh, as seamen lay in
store of beef for a long voyage.

On the Mechanical Operation of the Spirit, 1704

There is a very good word, which hath of late suffered much by both parties; I mean Moderation; which the one side [Rome] very justly disowns, and the other [the Presbytery] as unjustly pretends to.

Sentiments of a Church of England Man, with
Respect to Religion and Government, 1708

Are fewer claps got upon Sundays than other days?
Argument Against Abolishing Christianity, 1708

I confess, if it were certain that so great an advantage would redound to the nation by this expedient I would submit and be silent. But will any man say that if the words whoring, drinking, cheating, lying, stealing, were by act of parliament ejected out of the English tongue and dictionaries, we should all awake next morning chaste and temperate, honest and just, and lovers of truth? *ibid.*

I wish you a merry Lent. I hate Lent; I hate different diets, and furmity and butter, and herb porridge; and sour devout faces of people who only put on religion for seven weeks.

Journal to Stella, 5 March 1712

The word conscience properly signifies that knowledge which a man hath within himself of his own thoughts and actions. And because if a man judgeth fairly of his own actions by comparing them with the law of God, his mind will either approve or condemn him according as he hath done good or evil; therefore this knowledge or conscience may properly be called both an accuser and a judge. So that whenever our conscience accuseth us, we are certainly guilty; but we are not always innocent when it doth not accuse us.

The Testimony of Conscience: a sermon, after 1713

That a religious conscience is necessary in any station, is confessed even by those who tell us that all religion was invented by cunning men in order to keep the world in awe.

ibid.

It is very possible for a man who hath the appearance of religion, and is a great pretender to conscience, to be wicked and an hypocrite; but it is impossible for a man who openly declares against religion to give any reasonable security that he will not be false or cruel, and corrupt, whenever a temptation offers which he values more than he does the power wherewith he was trusted.

ibid.

God sent us into the world to obey his commands, by doing as much good as our abilities will reach, and as little evil as our many infirmities will permit.

Duty of Mutual Subjection: a sermon, after 1713

A man truly moderate is steady in the doctrine and discipline of the Church, but with a due Christian charity to all who dissent from it out of principle of conscience; the freedom of which, he thinketh, ought to be fully allowed, as long as it is not abused, but never trusted with power ... A moderate man, in the new meaning of the word, is one to whom all religion is indifferent, who, although he denominateth himself of the Church, regardeth it no more than a conventicle.

Brotherly Love: a sermon, 1 December 1717

That this indecent sloth is very much owing to that luxury and excess men usually practise upon this day, by which half the service thereof is turned into sin; men dividing their time between God and their bellies, when after a gluttonous meal, their sense dozed and stupefied, they retire to God's house to sleep out the afternoon. Surely, Brethren, these things ought not to be.

A Sermon Upon Sleeping in Church, c. 1720

Philosophy & Science

The stoical scheme of supplying our wants by lopping off our desires, is like cutting off our feet, when we want shoes.

Thoughts on Various Subjects

Physicians ought not to give their judgment of religion, for the same reason that butchers are not admitted to be jurors upon life and death.

ibid.

The greatest inventions were produced in the times of ignorance; as the use of the compass, gunpowder, and printing; and by the dullest nation, as the Germans.

ibid.

Apollo was held the God of Physick, and sender of diseases: both were originally the same trade, and still continue.

ibid.

Philosophy! the lumber of the schools.

'Ode to Sir William Temple', 1692

The philosopher's way in all ages has been by erecting certain edifices in the air. But, whatever practice and reputation these kind of structures have formerly possessed, or may still continue in, not excepting even that of Socrates, when he was suspended in a basket to help contemplation; I think, with due submission, they seem to labour under two inconveniences. First, that the foundations being laid too high, they have been often out of sight, and ever out of hearing. Secondly, that the materials, being very transitory, have suffered much from inclemencies of air, especially in these North-West regions.

A Tale of a Tub I, 1704

He had been eight years upon a project for extracting
sun-beams from cucumbers, which were to be put into
vials hermetically sealed, and let out to warm the air in
raw inclement summers ... We next went to the school
of languages, where three professors sat in consultation
upon improving that of their own country. The first
project was to shorten discourse by cutting polysyllables
into one, and leaving out verbs and participles, because
in reality all things imaginable are but nouns. The other
project was a scheme for entirely abolishing all words
whatsoever; and this was urged as a great advantage in
point of health as well as brevity. For it is plain, that
every word we speak is in some degree a diminution of
our lungs by corrosion, and consequently contributes to
the shortening of our lives.

Gulliver's Travels III, 1726

There is nothing so extravagant and irrational which
some philosophers have not maintained for truth.

ibid.

[Aristotle] freely acknowledged his own mistakes in
natural philosophy, because he proceeded in many
things upon conjecture, as all men must do ... He said,
that new systems of nature were but new fashions,
which would vary in every age; and even those who
pretended to demonstrate them from mathematical
principles would flourish but a short period of time, and
be out of vogue when that was determined.

ibid.

Hobbes clearly proves that every creature
Lives in a state of war by nature.

'On Poetry: A Rhapsody', 1733

The best doctors in the world are Doctor Diet, Doctor
Quiet, and Doctor Merryman.

Polite Conversation 2, 1738

Politics

The two maxims of any great man at court are, always to keep his countenance, and never to keep his word.

Thoughts on Various Subjects

Censure is the tax a man pays to the public for being eminent.

ibid.

Princes in their infancy, childhood, and youth, are said to discover prodigious parts and wit; to speak things that surprise and astonish. Strange, so many hopeful princes, and so many shameful kings! If they happen to die young, they would have been prodigies of wisdom and virtue: if they live, they are often prodigies indeed, but of another sort.

ibid.

Party is the madness of many for the gain of a few.

ibid.

Arbitrary power is the natural object of temptation to a prince; as wine or women to a young fellow, or a bribe to a judge, or avarice to old age, or vanity to a female.

ibid.

Law, in a free country, is, or ought to be, the determination of the majority of those who have Property in Land.

ibid.

Praise is the daughter of present Power.

ibid.

The saying 'Vox populi vox Dei', ought to be understood of the universal bent and current of the people, not the bare majority of a few representatives; which is often procured by little arts, and great industry and application; wherein those who engage in the pursuits of malice and revenge, are much more sedulous than such as would prevent them.

Contests and Dissensions in Athens and Rome, 1701

When the balance of power is duly fixed in a state, nothing is more dangerous and unwise than to give way to the first steps of popular encroachments, which is usually done either in hopes of procuring ease and quiet from some vexatious clamour, or else made merchandise, and merely bought and sold. This is breaking into a constitution to serve a present expedient, or supply a present exigency.

ibid.

In all free states, the evil to be avoided is tyranny, that is to say, the *summa imperii,* or unlimited power solely in the hands of the One, the Few, or the Many.

ibid.

Let speculative men reason, or rather refine as they please; it ever will be true among us, that as long as men engage in public service upon private ends, and whilst all the pretences to a sincere Roman love of our country, are looked upon as an affectation, a foppery, or a disguise ... it will be safer to trust our property and constitution in the hands of such who have paid for their elections, than of those who have obtained them by servile flatteries of the people.

ibid.

Blessed revolution, which creates,
Divided hearts, united states.

'Verses said to be written upon the Union', 1707

Laws are like cobwebs, which may catch small flies, but let wasps and hornets break through.

A Tritical Essay upon the Faculties of the Mind, 1707

Interest governs the world, and men neglect the golden mean.

ibid.

To enter into a Party as into an order of friars, with so resigned an obedience to superiors, is very unsuitable both with the civil and religious liberties we so zealously assert.

Sentiments of a Church of England Man, 1708

There is one essential point wherein a political liar differs from the others of the faculty; that he ought to have but a short memory, which is necessary according to the various occasions he meets with every hour, of differing from himself, and swearing to both sides of a contradiction, as he finds the persons disposed, with whom he has to deal.

The Examiner XV, November 1710

It is usually reckoned a whig principle to appeal to the people; but that is only when they have been so wise as to poison their understanding beforehand.

The Examiner XXXII, March 1711

It is folly of too many to mistake the echo of a London coffee house for the voice of the kingdom.

The Conduct of the Allies, 1711

The art of government ... requires no more, in reality, than diligence, honesty, and a moderate share of plain natural sense.

An Enquiry into the Behaviour of the Queen's Last Ministry,
c. 1715-17

When I conversed among ministers, I boasted of your acquaintance, but I feel no vanity from being known to a Secretary of State. I am only a little concerned to see you stand single, for it is a prodigious singularity in any Court to owe one's rise entirely to merit. I will venture to tell you a secret, that three or four such choices, would gain more hearts in three weeks than all the methods hitherto practised have been able to do in as many years.

Letter to Joseph Addison, 9 July 1717

Liberty of conscience is nowadays not only understood to be the liberty of believing what men please, but also of endeavouring to propagate the belief as much as they can and to overthrow the faith which the laws have already established, to be rewarded by the public for those wicked endeavours.

The Testimony of Conscience: a sermon, after 1713

It is safer for a man's interest to blaspheme God than to be of a party out of power or even to be thought so.

Letter to Thomas Sheridan, 11 September 1725

All government without the consent of the governed is the very definition of slavery.

Drapier's Letters IV, 1725

And he gave it for his opinion, that whoever could make two ears of corn or two blades of grass to grow upon a spot of ground where only one grew before, would deserve better of mankind, and do more essential service to his country than the whole race of politicians put together.

Gulliver's Travels II, 1726

He likewise directed, that every senator in the great council of a nation, after he had delivered his opinion, and argued in the defence of it, should be obliged to give his vote directly contrary; because, if that were done, the result would infallibly terminate in the good of the public.

ibid., III

I was chiefly disgusted with modern history. For having strictly examined all the persons of greatest name in the courts of princes for an hundred years past, I found how the world had been misled by prostitute writers, to ascribe the greatest exploits in war to cowards, the wisest counsel to fools, sincerity to flatterers, Roman virtue to betrayers of their country, piety to atheists, chastity to sodomites, truth to informers ... Here I discovered the true causes of many great events that have surprised the world, how a whore can govern the back-stairs, the back-stairs a council, and the council a senate ... [T]he royal throne could not be supported without corruption, because the positive, confident, restive temper, which virtue infused into man, was a perpetual clog to public business [while] Perjury, oppression, subordination, fraud, pandarism, and the like infirmities were among the most excusable arts.

ibid., III

Poor nations are hungry, and rich nations are proud; and pride and hunger will ever be at variance.

ibid., IV

There is no talent so useful towards rising in the world, or which puts men more out of the reach of fortune than the quality generally possessed by the dullest sort of people, in common speech called discretion; a species of lower prudence, by the assistance of which, people of the meanest intellectuals, without any other qualification, pass through the world in great tranquillity, and with universal good treatment, neither giving nor taking offence. Courts are seldom unprovided of persons of this character.

The Intelligencer V, 1728

Whether hatred and violence between parties in a state be not more inflamed by different views of interest, than by the greater or lesser difference between them, either in religion or government?

Queries relating to the Sacramental Test, 1732

Ireland

A gentleman in the neighbourhood had two mistresses, another and myself; and he pretended honourable love to us both. Our three houses stood pretty near one another; his was parted from mine by a river, and from my rival's by an old broken wall.

The Story of the Injured Lady, being a true picture of Scotch
perfidy, Irish poverty and English partiality, 1707

[On Ireland:] I was reckoned to be as handsome as any of our neighbourhood, until I became pale and thin with grief and ill-usage ... Some years ago, this gentleman taking a fancy either to my person or my fortune, made his addresses to me; which, being then young and foolish, I too readily admitted ... All my constancy and virtue were too soon overcome; and ... I must confess with shame, that I was undone by the common arts practised upon all easy credulous virgins, half by force and half by consent, after solemn vows and protestations of marriage. When he had once got possession, he soon began to play the usual part of a too fortunate lover, affecting on all occasions to shew his authority, and to act like a conqueror.

ibid.

I reckon no man is thoroughly miserable unless he be condemned to live in Ireland.

Letter to Ambrose Philips, 30 October 1709

I must be bold to say, that people in this kingdom do very ill understand raillery. I can rally much safer here [in England] with a great minister of state or a duchess, than I durst there with an attorney or his wife.

Letter to Archbishop King, 10 April 1711

Ireland is not a paradise.

Letter to Alexander Pope, 30 August 1716

A great cause of this nation's misery, is that Egyptian bondage of cruel, oppressing, covetous landlords, expecting that all who live under them should make bricks without straw, who grieve and envy when they see a tenant of their own in a whole coat, or able to afford one comfortable meal in a month, by which the spirits of the people are broken.

On the wretched Condition of Ireland: a sermon, c. 1720

It is certainly a bad scheme to any Christian country ... that there should be any beggars at all. But, alas! among us, where the whole nation itself is almost reduced to beggary by the disadvantages we lie under, and the hardships we are forced to bear; the laziness, ignorance, thoughtlessness, squandering temper, slavish nature, and uncleanly manner of living in the poor popish natives, together with the cruel oppressions of their landlords, who delight to see their vassals in the dust; I say, that in such a nation, how can we otherwise expect than to be overrun with objects of misery and want?

ibid.

It is a peculiar felicity and prudence of the people in this kingdom, that whatever commodities or productions lie under the greatest discouragements from England, those are what we are sure to be most industrious in cultivating ... Let a firm resolution be taken by male and female, never to appear with one single shred that comes from England. 'And let all the people say, Amen.'

A Proposal for the Universal Use of Irish Manufacture, 1720

Some ministries ... look down upon this kingdom as if it had been one of their colonies of outcasts in America.

ibid.

What would you do in these parts, where politeness is as much a stranger as cleanliness?

Letter to Esther Vanhomrigh, 7 August 1722

So, to confound this hated coin,
All parties and religions join;
Whigs, Tories, trimmers, Hanoverians,
Quakers, conformists, presbyterians,
Scotch, Irish, English, French unite
With equal interest, equal spite ...
A strange event! whom gold incites,
To blood and quarrels, brass unites.

> 'Prometheus (On Wood the Patentee's Irish Halfpence)', 1724

Am I a Free-man in England, and do I become a slave in
six hours, by crossing the Channel?

> *Drapier's Letters* III, 1724

Those who come over to us from England, and some
weak people among ourselves, whenever in discourse
we make mention of liberty and property, shake their
heads and tell us that Ireland is a 'depending kingdom',
as if they would seem, by this phrase, to intend that the
people of Ireland is in some state of slavery or
dependence different from those of England. Whereas a
'depending kingdom' is a modern term of art, unknown,
as I have heard, to all ancient civilians and writers upon
government ... I have looked over all the English and
Irish statutes without finding any law that makes
Ireland depend upon England, any more than England
does upon Ireland.

> *ibid.*, IV, 1724

I think it manifest that whatever circumstances can
possibly contribute to make a country poor and
despicable, are all united with respect to Ireland.

> Letter to the Earl of Peterborough, 28 April 1726

[T]he Yahoos appear to be the most unteachable of all animals, their capacities never reaching higher than to draw or carry burthens. Yet I am of opinion this defect ariseth chiefly from a perverse, restive disposition. For they are cunning, malicious, treacherous and revengeful. They are strong and hardy, but of a cowardly spirit, and by consequence insolent, abject, and cruel. It is observed that the red-haired of both sexes are more libidinous and mischievous than the rest, whom yet they much exceed in strength and activity.

Gulliver's Travels IV, 1726

It is too well known, that we are forced to obey some laws we never consented to ... As to improvement of land; those few who attempt this, or planting, through covetousness, or want of skill, generally leave things worse than they were ... We are so far from having a King to reside among us, that even the viceroy is generally absent four-fifths of his time in government. No strangers from other countries, make this a part of their travels; where they can expect to see nothing, but scenes of misery and desolation ... [Such a stranger] would be apt to think himself travelling in Lapland or Iceland, rather than in a country so favoured by nature as ours.

A Short View of the State of Ireland, 1727

Remove me from this land of slaves,
Where all are fools, and all are knaves;
Where every knave and fool is bought,
Yet kindly sells himself for naught.

'Ireland', 1727

I have been assured by a very knowing American of my acquaintance in London, that a young healthy child well nursed is at a year old a most delicious, nourishing, and wholesome food, whether stewed, roasted, baked, or boiled, and I make no doubt that it will equally serve in a fricassee, or a ragout.

A Modest Proposal for Preventing the Children of Ireland from being a Burden to their parents or country, 1729

You think, as I ought to think, that it is time for me to have done with this world, and so I would if I could get into a better before I was called into the best, and not die here in a rage, like a poisoned rat in a hole. I wonder you are not ashamed to let me pine away in this kingdom.

Letter to Viscount Bolingbroke, 21 March 1729

I will define Ireland a region of good eating and drinking, where a man from England may sojourn some years with pleasure, make a fortune, and then return home, with the spoils he has got by doing us all the mischief he can, and by that make a merit at court.

Letter to John Gay, 20 November 1729

Poor floating isle, tossed on ill fortune's waves,
Ordained by fate to be the land of slaves.

'Horace Book I, Ode XIV (Paraphrased and inscribed to Ireland)',
1730

A servile race in folly nursed
Who truckle most when treated worst.

'Verses upon the death of Dr Swift', 1731

I never yet saw in Ireland a spot of earth two feet wide, that had not in it something to displease ... [T]he whole kingdom [is] a bare face of nature, without houses or plantations; filthy cabins, miserable, tattered, half-starved creatures, scarce in human shape; one insolent, ignorant, oppressive squire to be found in twenty miles riding; a parish church to be found only in a summer-day's journey, in comparison of which, an English farmer's barn is a cathedral; a bog of fifteen miles round; every meadow a slough, and every hill a mixture of rock, heath, and marsh; and every male and female, from the farmer inclusive to the day-labourer, infallibly a thief, and consequently a beggar, which in this island are terms convertible ... There is not an acre of land in Ireland turned to half its advantage; yet it is better improved than the people: and all these evils are effects of English tyranny.

Letter to Dean Brandreth, 30 June 1732

It may be proper to give you a short state of our
unfortunate country. We consist of two parties, I do not
mean Popish and Protestant, High and Low Church,
Episcopal and Sectarian, Whig and Tory; but, of these,
English who happen to be born in this kingdom (whose
ancestors reduced the whole nation under the obedience
of the English crown) and the gentlemen sent from the
other side to possess most of the chief employments here.

Advice to the Freemen of Dublin, 1733

As I stroll the city, oft I
Spy a building large and lofty,
Not a bow-shot from the College,
Half a globe from sense and knowledge ...
Tell us, what this pile contains?
Many a head that holds no brains.

'A Character, Panegyric and description of the
Legion Club [the Irish Parliament]', 1736

Contemporaries

For never did poetic mine before
Produce a richer vein or cleaner ore;
The bullion stamped in your refining mind
Serves by retail to furnish half mankind.

'To William Congreve', 1693

[Dryden] has often said to me in confidence, that the
world would have never suspected him to be so great a
poet, if he had not assured them so frequently in his
Prefaces that it was impossible they could either doubt
or forget it.

A Tale of a Tub V, 1704

[On Daniel Defoe:] So grave, sententious, dogmatical a
rogue, that there is no enduring him.

A Letter Concerning the Sacramental Test, 1708

He has three predominant passions which you will
seldom observe united in the same man, as arising from
different dispositions of mind, and naturally thwarting
each other: these are love of power, love of money, and
love of pleasure. They ride him sometimes by turns and
sometimes all together.

A Short Character of Thomas, Earl of Wharton, 1710

[Robert Harley] The Earl of Oxford is a person of as
much virtue, as can possibly consist with the love of
power ... He is the only instance that ever fell within my
memory, or observation, of a person passing from a
private life, through the several stages of greatness,
without any perceivable impression upon his temper
and behaviour.

*An Enquiry into the behaviour of the Queen's
Last Ministry*, 1715-17

[On John Gay's *The Beggar's Opera*, the idea for which Swift may have suggested:] Nothing but servile attachment to a party, affection of singularity, lamentable dullness, mistaken zeal, or studied hypocrisy, can have the least reasonable objection against this excellent moral performance.

The Intelligencer, 25 May 1728

The truest, most virtuous, and valuable friend, that I, or perhaps any other person ever was blessed with ... I cannot call to mind that I ever once heard her make a wrong judgment of persons, books, or affairs. Her advice was always the best, and with the greatest freedom, mixed with the greatest decency ... Never was so happy a conjunction of civility, freedom, easiness and sincerity.

On the death of Mrs Esther Johnson, 1728

With favour and fortune fastidiously blest,
He's loud in his laugh, and he's coarse in his jest:
Of favour and fortune unmerited, vain,
A sharper in trifles, a dupe in the main.
Achieving of nothing – still promising wonders –
By dint of experience improving in blunders.
Oppressing true merit, exalting the base,
And selling his country to purchase his place ...
Though I name not the wretch, yet you know whom I
    mean –
'Tis the cur-dog of Britain, and spaniel of Spain.

'A Character of Sir Robert Walpole', 1731

I could not live with my Lord Bolingbroke or Mr Pope: they are both too temperate and too wise for me, and too profound and too poor.

Letter to John Arbuthnot, November 1734

[On Isaac Newton:] The man it seems was knighted for making sun-dials better than others of his trade, and was thought to be a conjuror, because he knew how to draw lines and circles upon a slate, which nobody could understand.

Polite Conversation, 1738

In Pope, I cannot read a line,
But with a sigh, I wish it mine:
When he can in one Couplet fix
More sense than I can do in six:
It gives me such a jealous fit,
I cry, 'Pox take him, and his wit.'

'Verses on the death of Doctor Swift', 1738-9

[On Handel:] Ah, a German and a genius! a prodigy,
admit him!

Attributed last words, 1745

Poetry, Oratory, Satire & Criticism

Positiveness is a good quality for preachers and orators, because he that would obtrude his thoughts and reasons upon a multitude, will convince others the more, as he appears convinced himself.

Thoughts on Various Subjects

Vision is the art of seeing things invisible.

ibid.

In oratory the greatest art is to hide art.

ibid.

The common fluency of speech in many men, and most women, is owing to a scarcity of matter, and a scarcity of words; for whoever is a master of language, and has a mind full of ideas, will be apt, in speaking, to hesitate upon the choice of both; whereas common speakers have only one set of ideas, and one set of words to clothe them in; and these are always ready at the mouth.

ibid.

Eloquence, smooth and cutting, is like a razor whetted with oil.

ibid.

Few are qualified to shine in company; but it is in most men's power to be agreeable. The reason, therefore, why conversation runs so low at present, is not the defect of understanding, but pride, vanity, ill nature, affectation, singularity, positiveness, or some other vice, the effect of a wrong education.

ibid.

All panegyrics are mingled with an infusion of poppy.

ibid.

Satire is a sort of glass, wherein beholders do generally discover everybody's face but their own.

The Battle of the Books, Preface, 1704

I have sometimes heard of an Iliad in a nutshell, but it hath been my fortune to have more oftener seen a nutshell in an Iliad.

A Tale of a Tub III, 1704

I conceive, therefore, as to the business of being profound, that it is with writers as with wells – a person with good eyes may see to the bottom of the deepest provided any water be there, and that often when there is nothing in the world at the bottom besides dryness and dirt, though it be but a yard and a half underground it shall pass, however, for wondrous deep, upon no wiser reason than because it is wondrous dark.

ibid., Conclusion

I am now trying an experiment very frequent among modern authors, which is to write upon nothing; when the subject is utterly exhausted, to let the pen still move on; by some called the ghost of wit, delighting to walk after the death of its body. And to say the truth, there seems to be no part of knowledge in fewer hands than that of discerning when to have done.

ibid.

I have one further favour to request of my reader; that he will not expect to be equally diverted and informed by every line or every page of this discourse, but give some allowance to the author's spleen and short fits or intervals of dullness, as well as his own; and lay it seriously to his conscience whether, if he were walking the streets in dirty weather or a rainy day, he would allow it fair dealing in folks at their ease from a window to critick his gait, and ridicule his dress at such a juncture.

ibid.

Great wits love to be free with the highest objects, and if they cannot be allowed a God to revile or renounce, they will speak evil of dignitaries, abuse the government, and reflect upon the ministry.

Argument against Abolishing Christianity, 1708

Men would be more cautious of losing their time in [criticism], if they did but consider that to answer a book effectually requires more pains and skill, more wit, learning, and judgment than were employed in the writing it.

'An Apology', *A Tale of a Tub*, 1709

Proper words in proper places, makes the true definition of a style.

Letter to a young gentleman lately entered into Holy Orders, 1720

[Satire is] a public spirit, prompting men of genius and virtue, to mend the world as far as they are able.

The Intelligencer III, May 1728

And although some things are too serious, solemn, or sacred to be turned into ridicule, yet the abuses of them are certainly not, since it is allowed that corruption in religion, politics, and law, may be proper topics for ... satire.

ibid.

Say, Britain, could you ever boast, –
Three poets in an age at most?
Our chilling climate hardly bears
A sprig of bays in fifty years.

'On Poetry: A Rhapsody', 1733

Then, rising with Aurora's light,
The Muse invoked, sit down to write;
Blot out, correct, insert, refine,
Enlarge, diminish, interline.

ibid.

As learned commentators view
In Homer more than Homer knew.

ibid.

So, naturalists, observe a flea
Hath smaller fleas that on him prey;
And these have smaller fleas to bite 'em,
And so proceed ad infinitum.
Thus every poet, in his kind,
Is bit by him that comes behind.

ibid.

Old Age & Death

Not to marry a young woman.

Not to keep young company unless they really desire it.

Not to be peevish or morose, or suspicious.

Not to scorn present Ways, or Wits, or Fashions, or Men, or War, &c.

Not to be fond of children, or let them come near me hardly.

Not to tell the same story over and over to the same people.

Not to be covetous.

Not to neglect decency, or cleanliness, for fear of falling into nastiness.

Not to be over severe with young people, but give allowances for their youthful follies, and weaknesses.

Not to be influenced by, or give ear to knavish tattling servants, or others.

Not to be too free of advice, nor trouble any but those that desire it.

To desire some good Friends to inform me which of these resolutions I break, or neglect, and wherein; and reform accordingly.

Not to talk much, nor of myself.

Not to boast of my former beauty, or strength, or favour with ladies, &c.

Not to hearken to flatteries, nor conceive I can be beloved by a young woman, *et eos qui hereditatem captant, odisse ac vitare.*

Not to be positive or opinionative.

Not to set up for observing all these rules; for fear I should observe none.

When I Come to be Old, 1699

No preacher is listened to but Time, which gives us the same train and turn of thought that elder people have in vain tried to put into our heads before.

Thoughts on Various Subjects

Invention is the talent of youth, and judgment of age; so that our judgment grows harder to please, when we have fewer things to offer it: this goes through the whole commerce of life. When we are old our friends find it difficult to please us, and are less concerned whether we be pleased or no.

ibid.

No wise man ever wished to be younger.

ibid.

Every man desires to live long; but no man would be old.

ibid.

Dignity, high station, or great riches, are in some sort necessary to old men, in order to keep the younger at a distance, who are otherwise too apt to insult them upon the score of their age.

ibid.

Old men and comets have been reverenced for the same reason; their long beards, and pretences to foretell events.

ibid.

Observation is an old man's memory.

ibid.

Old men view best at a distance with the eyes of their understanding, as well as with those of nature.

ibid.

If a man would register all his opinions upon love, politics, religion, learning, &c. beginning from his youth, and so go on to old age, what a bundle of inconsistencies would appear at last?

ibid.

When I was young, I thought all the world, as well as
myself, was wholly taken up in discoursing upon the
last new play.

ibid.

The death of a private man is generally of so little
importance to the world, that it cannot be a thing of
great importance in itself; and yet I do not observe, from
the practice of mankind, that either philosophy or nature
have sufficiently armed us against the fears which attend
it. Neither do I find anything able to reconcile us to it,
but extreme pain, shame, or despair; for poverty,
imprisonment, ill-fortune, grief, sickness, and old age,
do generally fail.

ibid.

If a man will observe as he walks the streets, I believe he
will find the merriest countenances in mourning coaches.

ibid.

How blessed is he, who for his country dies;
Since death pursues the coward as he flies.

'To the Earl of Oxford, Late Lord Treasurer', *c.* 1716

The Earl of Godolphin is dead, and his faults may
sojourn with him in the grave till some historian shall
think fit to revive part of them for instruction and
warning to posterity.

The Importance of the Guardian Considered, 1713

When I was of your age I often thought of death, but
now, after a dozen years more, it is never out of my
mind, and terrifies me less. I conclude that Providence
has ordered our fears to decrease with our spirits.

Letter to Lord Bolingbroke, 21 March 1729

I shall be like that tree, I shall die at the top.

Attrib.

Swift's Epitaph

Hic depositum est Corpus
JONATHAN SWIFT S.T.D.
Hujus Ecclesiae Cathedralis
Decani,
Ubi saeva Indignatio
Ulterius
Cor lacerare nequit.
Abi Viator
Et imitare, si poteris,
Strenuum pro virili
Libertatis Vindicatorem.

Obiit 19 Die Mensis Octobris
A.D. 1745. Anno AEtatis 78.

[Here is laid the body of Jonathan Swift, Doctor of
Sacrosanct Theology, Dean of this cathedral church,
where savage indignation can no longer tear his heart.
Go, traveller, and imitate him if you can, a man who to
his utmost championed liberty.]

Swift has sailed into his rest;
Savage indignation there
Cannot lacerate his breast.
Imitate him if you dare,
World besotted traveller; he
Served human liberty.

W.B. Yeats, 'Swift's Epitaph', 1930